Seeds And Potter

Sakthi

First Published in 2021

Becomeshakespeare.com

One Point Six Technologies Pvt Ltd

119-123, 1st Floor, Building J2, B-Wing,
Wadala Truck Terminal, Wadala (East),
Mumbai 400022, Maharashtra, India

T: +91 8080226699

ISBN - 978-93-5438-721-0

To my friends

Sangeetha, Isha and Amit

Table of contents

Table of contents

I

Learning

Seeds and potter

Four walls of class room

Confining children to

A

Room

Like growing

Banyan tree in

A pot

Pot maker makes the

Pots with his own design

Does that fit

All seeds in

Classroom

Each seed is unique

Though they grow

Together

If they put up in

Same pot

Same room

Is there a room

For their expression

Freedom of expression

Never comes with freedom

It is confined to classroom

It is confined to potter design

Does the potter aware of his own design?

Patterns in design?.

The more potter looks at his own

Design

Closely

The closer

He knows the seeds

Seeds and potter are not

Different

In fact potter needs the seeds

To sell his pots

But seeds never in need of potter

It can grow wildly

Because

Every seed already has design

Within itself

For it's fullest expression

No one can

Take away

Seeds freedom

Potter can delay with his

Pot design

When potter seeks

Freedom

Seeds show the way

Let potter free himself first

Then he can design pot for

The seeds

Seeds never in need of potter

But the potter is

First step

First step in teaching is
To understand
How learning happens

First step to understand
How learning happens is
To be the learner

First step to be the learner is
To be the observer

First step to be the observer is
To step back and watch

First step to be the observer is
To step back and watch

Learning

Learning in

The world

Is it

Child driven

Or

Adult driven?

If it is

Child driven

Learning happens

Naturally

If it is

Adult driven

Learning happens

Unnaturally

Naturally

The child is

Curious

Playful

Adventurous

And much more

Unnaturally

The adult is

Dull

Boring

Repetition of old

And much less

Which one do you choose

Child driven

Or

Adult driven

Self driven

Or

Society driven

Teaching

Teaching

Is

To

Learn

How

To

Teach

Learn

How

To

Teach

By

Learning in

Teaching

Every

Learning

In

Teaching

Is

To

Teach

How

To

Teach

You

Learn

To

Teach

By

Learning

In

Teaching

You

Learn

How

To

Teach

Teaching

By

Learning the

Learning

In

Teaching

Framework

Within the framework
Need to work with in the framework
Need to work with in the framework that
Doesn't fit into any frame work

Framework that doesn't fit into any framework
Is that possible?
I ask myself.

If so then how?

If framework is fixed
Forever
Then that framework is not
Forever

Forever change happens
Change always change
So framework always need to change

Framework that doesn't fit into any framework

Is that possible?

21

It is possible when

Framework is not forever

It accepts changes forever

It is possible when

Framework is not forever

It accepts changes forever

Then that framework remains forever

Then that framework remains forever

Self discovery

One care taker for many caring ones

Everyone is on their own journey

Care taker

And

Many caring ones

They come together in a classroom

For a self discovery

Care taker for his self discovery

Caring ones for their self discovery

If care taker is in self discovery

Then caring ones are also in their self discovery

They discover their own path to discover their self

To discover the self they need

To discover their own path on their own

To discover the self they need

To discover their path on their own

Care taker his path

Caring ones their path

Space and time

To do

Self directed learning

To discover their path on their own

To discover their self

What they need to do?

They need to do

Self directed learning

To do self directed learning

They need to be in touch with their self

To be in touch with their self

They need space and free time for their self

To get space and free time for their self

They need to free their space and free their time

From busy space

From busy time

25

To get space and free time for their self

They need to free their space and free their time

From busy space

From busy time

Practice

Self directed learning in existing school structure

In 1 hour

30 mins of class room

30 mins of free time

30 mins teacher decides what children going to learn in a self directed way

30 mins children decides their own way

Doing this

Children discover their own potential by what they like to do any given moment

Any given moment they own up their choice, So the learning
As doing this way

Teacher discover his potential to work with the children who
really in need of help

Teacher discover his potential to create an environment
where being is learning

An environment where just being is learning
Then learning is joyful
Then learning is playful
Then learning is spontaneous

Once we see this happen in practice
So we trust the practice.

Once we see this happen in practice
So we trust the practice.

Being is learning

How to create an environment where being is learning

To create an environment where being is learning

We need to create an environment for just being

Being with themselves

Mixed age group, multiple activities, multiple choice for children to choose

Children choose their choice from multiple available choice

To create a multiple choice, we need a multiple thinkers, each children is a thinker along with teacher

So multiple choice for multiple people

Each one choose their choice based on their interest

On their interest they choose, with their interest they learn
29

On their interest they choose, with their interest they learn

Each one choose their choice based on their interest

Evaluation

How do you comprehend how learning happens?

By evaluation?

Before the evaluation we need to know how learner learnt what he actually learnt

To know how learner learnt
What learner learnt
Is that easy to comprehend?

How a bird learn to fly
How a fish learn to swim
How a child learn to talk
Learnt to master
The language
Learn to faster it's
Learning

Is that easy to understand

Is that easy to comprehend

Or it is come with a trust

Children, human beings are naturally curious

Natural learners

They learn as and when they feel the need to learn

what they have to learn

They learn as and when they feel the need to learn

what they have to learn

But only when they feel the need to learn

They learn only when

they need to learn their learning

II

Purpose

Foundation

How you initiate intuition

While you do tuition

Intuition is in roots

Tuition is in branches

Tree can't grow to its

True size if either one is missing

Foundation is roots

Foundation is intuition

Building is branches

Building is tuition

To keep foundation strong you need to dig

Deep

Within you

So within children

To keep foundation strong you need to dig

Deep

Within you

So within children

What about building?

Building is naturally strong

If foundation is strong

Building is unnaturally wrong

If foundation is wrong

Being and doing

Being and doing
While growing

While growing
Be and do

Just be for sometime
Do for sometime

If you are
Lost in doing
Or
Lost in being
You are lost
You are too fast

Be slow
In being

Be slow

In doing

In

Being and doing

You

Can be slow

Can be fast

In

Being and doing

You

Can be slow

Can be fast

Tutoring

Tutoring
Tuition

Tutoring
Intuition

While you initiate
Tuition you can also
Initiate intuition

Tuition you change them from
Who they are
Intuition you accept them
As they are

Who they are depends on
Who you are

Are you a tutor of tuition?

Are you a tutor of intuition?

Expansion

Can a self discovery happen

While in expansion

Village to mass city

Child to adult

Can a tree flower

While it is growing

How it is possible?

Flowering happens after the growth

Child to Adult

Plant to Tree

Flowering can happen while growing

While growing

Flowering can happen

If tree in expansion of

Roots not of branches

If child in touch with child within

Flowering can happen

While growing

Flowering can happen

While growing

Real education

What is education?

What is the true purpose of education?

If it is to prepare children for the life,

Then just learning about so many subjects and skills are enough?

Does that enough to face the life?

The difficulties of life?

Life is difficult

It always challenges us

It takes us out of our comfort zone every now and then

Does schools, learning spaces, parents and society prepare us for that?

To face the difficult situations

Emotional disturbances

Inner turmoils

Psychological sufferings

If education is to prepare children for the life

To face the life

Why we are not learning the important lesson of how to face
the life with all its ups and downs

To face the life with all its complexities

Real education is learn to meet life's challenges

To meet life challenges what we need to learn?

More understanding of external world

Or

More understanding of our inner world

More understanding of external world all over the world

But understanding of internal world

Our own thought processes

Habitual mind patterns

Awareness of all our actions

Is far less in our world

45

Either you like it or not

Whoever wherever you are in the world

Life doesn't leave you alone

You need to deal with yourself when difficulties arise

The important lesson one needs to learn

Is

How to deal with one self

How to solve the war we have with our own self

Our own true self

If education is to prepare children for the life,

Then just learning about so many subjects and skills are enough?

Right now

Freedom or discipline

Structure or non structure

Following routine or free flowing

Everything has its place

Everything has its pros and cons

In the world

Everything has its place

That's why they exist

The concept of good and bad

Has its place

Following good habits and avoiding bad habits have its place

In the world all the

Polarities have their place

Right or left have their place

Honouring them for what they are
And striking the balance
Not sticking to one routine or the other
Not following the same habitual mind pattern
Forever
Is more important

Consciously aware of our mind patterns and
Changing and challenging the patterns occasionally
Holds the key

The key is to be honest of
Aware of
Where you are at any given point in time
What you are drawn to any point in time

And then
Choosing the right choice for your needs

Nothing in excess holds the key for the success

The key is to be honest with yourself

Aware of yourself

Where you are right now

Wherever you are right now

Aware of your self

Aware of your true self

Wherever you are

You are always there

Wherever you are

Right now is always there

Here or there

You and

Right now is always there

Ever

Right now is only there

III

Dear teachers

Dear Teachers

Dear Teachers
If you have not
Been the moon
That reflects
On the water

Or if you have not
Been the lake
Where water and moon
Meets

Then you missed to gift
A spring to the flowers
That blossoms before you
And let the fragrance
Spread through class room
That freshens you
And
Your dear children

You cannot see

You cannot see
The students

Students cannot see
A teacher

You can see
Children

Children can see
You
As
One who Cares
One who Loves
One who knows

They are not
Students

You are not

Teacher

You are simply a being

That can see

Without labels

Without concepts

That can see

And

Do everything with

Love.

Star

Spreading million smiles

Of million stars

In classrooms

In schools

How can you spread

Million smiles of

Million stars inside the

Concrete walls?

What can I do?

The question stares at me whenever

I enter my classroom

Tired of trying

Different methods

Different formulas

Nothing worked to bring smile on

Our stars

55

To bring smile on our stars

To bring joy in the classroom

To bring life in schools

Let stars be stars

Instead of I be a star

Instead of I be a show

In stars show

Letting stars show

How to smile like a star

How to shine like a star

If I be a one among stars

I can become a star

If I be a one among stars

I can become a star

Land of children

Being with children is like a
Seed sower

You are throwing the seeds to the land of children
The land absorbs the seeds and keeps it within itself

Seeds may sprout or may not sprout right away
You don't have a say over it
Forcing it to sprout, you spoil the nature of the land
The land of children
But don't forget to sow the seeds
The seeds of good quality

Don't ever forget that
When you are with children
You are a seed sower

When it sprouts depends on many unknown factors
Depends on the nature of the seed

Depends on the nature of the land

But everything never sprouts before it's time

Everything has its own time and space to grow

Being patient is what we need to know

Being patient is what we need to show

Seed sower and the land of children are not different

They both are part of nature's design

Nature's plan for cultivation

If you are a seed sower

You may think it's you who plan and does cultivation

But actually not

Your plan is innate part of nature's plan

If your plan not align with nature's plan

However whatever you throw never ever grow

Align your plan with nature's plan

Align yourself with nature

Then you are part of unknown plans of nature

As you become the nature

As you

Be your true nature

You may know the plan behind the unknown plan

To know the plan behind the unknown plan of nature

Of universe

Be your true nature

Your true nature is universe

You are the universe

Magic

Have

You

Seen

A

Cycle

That

Grows and

Shrinks

By

Magic

Have

You

Seen

A

Boy

Who

Has

That

Magical

Cycle

Have

You

Seen

That

Magical boy

With that

Magical cycle

If

You

See

Him

See

The

Magic

Not the boy

Not the cycle

See

The

Magic

Not the boy

Not the cycle

Hurry up

Hurry up

Hurry up

Time is

Running

Out

Hurry up

Hurry up

Time is

Running

Out

Where are

We

Going

I tell you

Later

Hurry up

Hurry up

Time

Is

Running

Out

Running for

What?

I tell

You

Later

You always

Tell

Later

Latter

Also

You tell

Latter

Latter

Now

It

Is

Late

Late for?

Not to be

Late

Why

Late?

I don't

Want to be

Late

I want to

Be ahead

Ahead for?

To go

Ahead

For what?

Not to be

Late

To go

Ahead

For

What?

Latter

Now

I need to

Hurry

To

Ahead

Now

Hurry up

Hurry up

Time is Running

Out

Serious

Are

You

Serious

About

Life

Life

Needs

To

Dealt

With

Lot of

Seriousness

Without

Seriousness

You can't

Achieve

Anything

Without

Seriousness

You'll

Be

One of

The

Losers

Don't

Lose

Your

Seriousness

Be

Serious

About

Seriousness

Be

Serious

About

Being

Serious

Being

Serious

Is

Very

Serious

So

Be

Very

Very

Serious

Be

Very

Very

Serious

Else

Serious

Lose

It's

Seriousness

Life

Lose

It's

Seriousness

Serious

Seriousness

It's

Seriousness

IV
Society

Well being

Interest of social well being

Comes with interest?

Or under compulsion?

Well being

Ever

Comes

Under compulsion?

Under compulsion

Interest comes?

Or

Disinterest comes?

Under compulsion

Interest comes?

Or

Disinterest comes?

Disinterest comes

When well being

Is not in interest

Disinterest comes

When well being

Is not in interest

Rest in peace

In our society
In our schools
Silence and empty spaces
Upset
Our teachers and
Us

The quick is the smart
The slow is the stupid

We like to fill every empty space and
Silence
With stuffs
All the time

All the time stuffs
Rest in peace
We say only in the end
Only when our time ends

We rarely at rest with peace

We rarely rest in peace when we live

To be at peace

To rest in peace when we live

Be comfortable with silence and empty space

Comparison

Who

Is

Blessed?

Who

Has

Knows

Posses

More?

Or

Less?

Who

Is

Blessed?.

Less

Is

Blessed

When Less

See

More is

Not

Blessed

More is

Blessed

When

Less see

It

Is not

Blessed

Less

Is

Less

When

Compared to

More

More

Is

Less

When

Compared to

More than

More

More than

More

Less than

Less

Are in

Comparison

When

Comparison

Is there

Who is

Blessed?

More

Comparison?

Or

Less

Comparison?

When

Comparison

Is there

Who is

Blessed?

More

Comparison?

Or

Less

Comparison?

Schools and marketing

Marketing offers
Offer lot of unnecessary offers

Unnecessary offers offer
Which we don't need
Which we don't want
Which we are not interested in

They try hard to convince us to take that offer
So much
So much
So so much much of
Unnecessary efforts

Children are the future of society
Children are the future society
We want to train them
From schools to market place
Market force for the market place

We force in schools

We train them

We take the role of marketing agents

Force them to take what they are not at all interested

They are not at all interested

If we force them

If we try to convince them for our own marketing benefits

Market force in schools

Schools for marketing are one and the same

They teach the same

They do the same

They offer lot of unnecessary offers

Unnecessary offers offer

Which we don't need

Which we don't want

Which we are not interested in

They try hard to convince us to take that offer

So much

So much

So so much much of

Unnecessary efforts

Society's business

Kids
Fashion
Show
Dance
Show
Reality
Show

Creating
Making
Fun of
Their
Innocence
For the
TRP rating

Everything
Is

Commodity

For the

TRP rating

For TRP rating

Make

Everything as

Commodity

Do our

Children are

Commodities?.

Do our

Children are

Commodities

For the

Society's

Businesses?

Do our

Children are

Commodities

For the

Society's

Businesses?